Michael ROSEN'S Book of Very Silly Poems

Illustrated by Shoo Rayner

PUFFIN

**Michael Rosen is a funny one,
He's got a nose like a pickled onion,
He's got a face like a squashed tomato,
And feet like fried fish.**

PUFFIN BOOKS

Published by the Penguin Group
Penguin Books Ltd, 80 Strand, London WC2R 0RL, England
Penguin Group (USA) Inc., 375 Hudson Street, New York, New York 10014, USA
Penguin Group (Canada), 90 Eglinton Avenue East, Suite 700, Toronto, Ontario, Canada M4P 2Y3
(a division of Pearson Penguin Canada Inc.)
Penguin Ireland, 25 St Stephen's Green, Dublin 2, Ireland (a division of Penguin Books Ltd)
Penguin Group (Australia), 250 Camberwell Road, Camberwell, Victoria 3124, Australia
(a division of Pearson Australia Group Pty Ltd)
Penguin Books India Pvt Ltd, 11 Community Centre, Panchsheel Park, New Delhi – 110 017, India
Penguin Group (NZ), 67 Apollo Drive, Rosedale, North Shore 0632, New Zealand
(a division of Pearson New Zealand Ltd)
Penguin Books (South Africa) (Pty) Ltd, 24 Sturdee Avenue, Rosebank, Johannesburg 2196, South Africa

Penguin Books Ltd, Registered Offices: 80 Strand, London WC2R 0RL, England

puffinbooks.com

First published by A & C Black (Publishers) Ltd 1994
Published in Puffin Books 1996
23

Text copyright © Michael Rosen, 1994
Illustrations copyright © Shoo Rayner, 1994
All rights reserved

The moral right of the author and illustrator has been asserted

Made and printed in England by Clays Ltd, St Ives plc

British Library Cataloguing in Publication Data
A CIP catalogue record for this book is available from the British Library

ISBN: 978-0-140-37137-6

www.greenpenguin.co.uk

Penguin Books is committed to a sustainable future
for our business, our readers and our planet.
The book in your hands is made from paper
certified by the Forest Stewardship Council.

Contents

Mega Monstrosities

Riotous Relatives

Verbal Burble

Neverending Narratives

Festering Food

Gunerania's wedding cake

The king he baked a wedding cake upon a sunny
day,
The king he baked a wedding cake, it was in the
month of May,
The king he baked a wedding cake, he filled it
with old clocks,
A cabbage, and an octopus, some apples and red
socks.
He mixed it, he whisked it, he threw it on the floor,
He crushed it, he mushed it, and it slithered out the
door.

The king he baked a wedding cake and the glue he
used was runny,
The king he baked a wedding cake with spiders and
some honey,
The king he baked a wedding cake, he filled it with
rusty nails,
A crocodile, a felt-tip pen, and a pinch of powdered
snails.
He folded it, he moulded it, he squeezed it through his
toes,
He sliced it, and diced it, 'til the flour went up his nose.

The king he baked a wedding cake, he added ripe
    bananas,
The king he baked a wedding cake, it was striped
    like his pyjamas,
The king he baked a wedding cake, it was sixty-one
    feet high,
It weighed ten tons, it squashed his thumbs, which
    made the poor king cry.
He iced it, he sliced it, he packed it with black slugs,
He covered it in manky moss, and a crust of orange
    bugs.

The king he baked a wedding cake with rats and
    cats and bats,
The·king he baked a wedding cake with a thousand
    buzzing gnats,
The king he baked a wedding cake, he gave it to
    the queen,
It made her sick for fifty years and turned her blue
    and green.
She bashed him, she thrashed him, she hit him with a
    frog,
She swung him, she flung him, and slapped him with a
    log.

Robert Soulsby and class 1S, Brookvale Junior School

'Neath the crust of the old apple pie

'Neath the crust of the old apple pie
There is something for you and for I;
It may be a pin that the cook has dropped in,
Or it may be a dear little fly, (dear little fly).
It may be an old rusty nail,
Or a piece of dear puppy dog's tail,
But whatever it be, it's for you and for me,
'Neath the crust of the old apple pie.

Traditional North American

Quick, quick

Quick, quick,
The cat's been sick,
Where, where,
Under the stair,
Hasten, hasten,
Fetch a basin,
Alas alack, 'tis all in vain,
Pussy's eaten it up again.

Traditional

School dinners

School dinners,
School dinners,
Iron beans,
Iron beans,
Sloppy semolina,
Sloppy semolina,
I feel sick,
Get a bowl quick.

Traditional

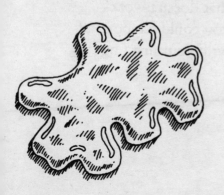

Peanut butter

There are three ways
to get peanut butter off
the roof of your mouth:

 One way is to shake your
head back and forth.

 If that doesn't work,
you could kind of whistle.

 If that doesn't work,
you could scrape it off
with your first finger.

There are three ways
  to get peanut butter off
  your finger.

 One way is to shake it off.

 Another way is to blow it off.

 If that doesn't work,
  you can scrape it off
  with your two front teeth.

There are three ways
  to get peanut butter off
  the roof of your mouth . . .

Traditional

13

Clothes
for Clots

I can't do my bally bottom button up

I can't do my bally bottom button up,
Can't do my bally bottom button up.
It's so tight, serves me right,
I must have eaten too much grub last night.
I can't do my bally bottom button up,
And though you think it's fun,
What's the use of buttoning the other bally
    buttons,
When the bally bottom button's undone?

J. P. Long

Black socks

Black socks, they never get dirty,
The longer you wear them the stronger they get.
Sometimes I think I should wash them,
But something inside me keeps saying,
'Not yet, not yet, not yet, not yet, not yet.'

Traditional

Undressed

We're walking through the air,
I've lost my underwear,
I'm going to Mothercare
to buy another pair
to wear . . .

Anon

Personal
Peculiarities

Do your ears hang low?

Do your ears hang low?

Do they wobble to and fro?

Can you tie them in a knot?

Can you tie them in a bow?

Can you throw them over your shoulder

Like a regimental soldier?

Do your ears hang low?

Do your ears hang high?

Do they wave up in the sky?

Do they crinkle when they're wet?

Do they straighten when they're dry?

Can you wave them at your neighbour

With a minimum of labour?

Do your ears hang high?

Traditional

Nobody loves me, everybody hates me

Nobody loves me, everybody hates me,
Guess I'll go and eat worms,
Long slim slimy ones, short fat juicy ones,
Itsy bitsy fuzzy wuzzy worms.

First you cut the heads off, then you suck the guts
    out,
Oh, how they wiggle and squirm,
Long slim slimy ones, short fat juicy ones,
Itsy bitsy fuzzy wuzzy worms.

Wiggle goes the first one, goosh goes the second
    one,
Sure don't wanna eat these worms,
Long slim slimy ones, short fat juicy ones,
Itsy bitsy fuzzy wuzzy worms.

Down goes the first one, down goes the second
    one,
Sure hate the taste of worms,
Long slim slimy ones, short fat juicy ones,
Itsy bitsy fuzzy wuzzy worms.

Nobody hates me, everybody likes me,
Never should've eaten those worms,
Long slim slimy ones, short fat juicy ones,
Itsy bitsy fuzzy wuzzy worms.

Up comes the first one, up comes the second one,
Oh, how they wiggle and squirm,
Long slim slimy ones, short fat juicy ones,
Itsy bitsy fuzzy wuzzy worms.

Traditional

I love to do my homework

I love to do my homework,
   it makes me feel so good,
I love to do exactly as the teacher
   says I should.
I love to do my schoolwork,
   I love it ev'ry day,
And I also love these men in white
   who are taking me away.

Traditional

Bugs go wild, simply wild, over me

Bugs go wild, simply wild, over me,
I'm referring to the bedbugs and the fleas.
Every morning, noon, and night all the bugs
    how they do bite,
Bugs go wild, simply wild, over me.

In the morning on my pillowcase
A daddy-long-legs stares me in the face,
In my underpants and shoes they assemble
    for a snooze,
Bugs go wild, simply wild, over me.

When I sit down to rest on a hike,
There are ants running left, running right,
There are spiders in my hair and mosquitoes
    everywhere,
Bugs go wild, simply wild, over me.

Traditional

Amazing Animals

In Frisco Bay there lives a whale

In Frisco Bay there lives a whale
And she eats peanuts by the pail,
And washtubs, and bathtubs, and sailboats,
  and schooners.

Her name is Sara and she's a peach
But don't leave food within her reach,
Or babies, or nursemaids, or chocolate
  ice cream sodas.

She loves to smile, and when she smiles
You can see her teeth for miles and miles,
And her tonsils, and her spare ribs,
  and things too fierce to mention.

She knows no games, so when she plays
She rolls her eyes for days and days,
She vibrates and yodels and breaks
  the Ten Commandments.

Now what you gonna do in a case like that?
There's nothing to do but sit on your hat,
Or your toothbrush, or your best friend,
  or anything else that's useless.

Traditional North American

A G-nu

I'm a G-nu, I'm a G-nu,
The g-nicest work of g-nature in the zoo!
I'm a G-nu, how do you do?
You really ought to k-now w-ho's w-ho.
I'm a G-nu, spelt G. N. U.
I'm g-not a camel or a kangaroo,
So let me introduce,
I'm g-neither man or moose,
Oh, g-no, g-no, g-no,
I'm a G-nu!

I'm a G-nu, ag-nother G-nu,
I wish I could g-nash my teeth at you,
I'm a G-nu, how do you do?
You really ought to k-now w-ho's w-ho.
I'm a G-nu, spelt G.N.U.
Call me bison or okapi and I'll sue,
G-nor am I in the least
Like that dreadful hartebeest
Oh, g-no, g-no, g-no,
I'm a G-nu!

Michael Flanders

Three craws sat upon a wa'

Three craws sat upon a wa',
Sat upon a wa',
Sat upon a wa' - a' - a' - a',
Three craws sat upon a wa'
On a cold and frosty morning.

The first craw couldnae flee at a',
Couldnae flee at a',
Couldnae flee at a' - a' - a' - a',
The first craw couldnae flee at a'
On a cold and frosty morning.

The second craw fell and broke his jaw,
Fell and broke his jaw,
Fell and broke his jaw - aw - aw - aw,
The second craw fell and broke his jaw
On a cold and frosty morning.

The third craw went and told his maw,
Went and told his maw,
Went and told his maw - aw - aw - aw,
The third craw went and told his maw
On a cold and frosty morning.

The fourth craw wisnae there at a',
Wisnae there at a',
Wisnae there at a' - a' - a' - a',
The fourth craw wisnae there at a'
On a cold and frosty morning.

Traditional Scottish

Nel and Ned

Big Nell and Ned,
The elephant pair,
Started to climb
Noah's wooden stair.
Stepped on the back,
Why I do declare,
The front of the ark
Shot up in the air.
    Poor old Nell and Ned. Boo hoo hoo!
    Far too heavy for Noah's Ark,
    What will old Noah do?

They both came up
For a second time,
On the left hand side
Decided to climb.
Left side went low,
Right side went high,
Shot all the animals,
Into the sky.
    Poor old Nell and Ned. Boo hoo hoo!
    Far too heavy for Noah's Ark,
    What will old Noah do?

Then Mrs Noah
Said, 'Please pay heed,
An equal balance
Is all you need.
Put Nell one end,
Balance Ned on the other,
Then the Ark will float
In the flood no bother.'
   Lucky old Nell and Ned. This is true!
   Mrs Noah was good at maths –
   Knew exactly what to do!

Morag Blance

BIG
Boasts!

Sylvest

He's my big brother Sylvest.
WHAT'S HE GOT?
He's got a row of forty medals 'cross his chest.
BIG CHEST!
Don't push, don't shove, plenty of room for
    you and me.
He's got an arm like a leg. BIG LEG!
And a punch that'd sink a battleship,
BIG SHIP!
Takes all the army and the navy
To put the wind up
SYLVEST!

Traditional, collected by Michael Rosen

Wizz Kings

We three kings of Orient are,
One in a taxi,
One in a car,
One in a scooter,
Blowing his hooter,
Smoking a big cigar.

Traditional

The biggest aspidistra in the world

For years we had an aspidistra in a flower pot
On the what-not near the hat stand in the hall.
It didn't seem to grow, till one day our brother Joe
Had a notion that he'd make it strong and tall.
So he crossed it with an acorn from an oak tree
And he planted it against the garden wall.

It shot up like a rocket till it nearly touched the sky,
It's the biggest aspidistra in the world.
We couldn't see the top of it, it got so bloomin'
    high,
It's the biggest aspidistra in the world.
When father's had a skinful at his pub *The Bunch
    of Grapes*
He doesn't go all fighting mad and getting into
    scrapes –

You'll find him in his bear skin playing 'Tarzan of
    the Apes'
Up the biggest aspidistra in the world.

The tom cats and the moggies love to spend their
    evenings out
Up the biggest aspidistra in the world.
They all begin miaowing when the buds begin to
    sprout
From the biggest aspidistra in the world.
The dogs line up for miles and miles, a funny sight
    to see,
They sniff around for hours on end and wag their
    tails with glee,
So I've 'ad to put a notice up to say it's not a tree –
It's the biggest aspidistra in the world.

It's getting worn and weary and its leaves are
    turning grey,
It's the oldest aspidistra in the world.
So we water it with half a pint of Guinness
    every day,
It's the stoutest aspidistra in the world.
The Borough Council told us that we've got to
    chop it down,
It interferes with aeroplanes that fly above the
    town,
So we sold it to a wood yard for a lousy half a
    crown,
It's the biggest aspidistra in the world.

Jimmy Harper

Mega
Monstrosities

Are you pink and green?

Are you pink and green?
Are you totally obscene?
Can you pick your nose
With your stubby little toes?
Do your armpits smell?
Are you hairy there as well?
Do your teeth fall out?

Does your belly-button gleam?
Does it let off purple steam?
Is your earwax foul?
Does your stomach groan and growl?
Are your hands like jelly?
Do they wobble like your belly?
Do you look like me?

Trina Bose, Sara Isenberg, Martina Klich,
Rebecca Ryan and Sheetal Borhara,
Moss Hall Junior School

Hobble gobble wobble

It was a stormy night on a Christmas day,
As they fell awake on the Santa Fe.

The ship in the dock was at the end of its trip,
And the man on board was the captain of the ship.

The name of the man was old Ben Brown
And he played the ukelele with his trousers down.

Turkey, jelly and the ship's old cook
All jumped out of a recipe book.

The jelly wobbled, the turkey gobbled
And after them both the old cook hobbled.

Gobbler gobbled Hobbler's Wobbler,
Hobbler gobbled Wobbler's Gobbler.

Gobbly-gobbler gobbled Wobbly,
Hobbly-hobbler gobbled Gobbly.

Gobble gobbled Hobble's Wobble,
Hobble gobbled gobbled Wobble.

Gobble gobble wobble wobble
Hobble gobble wobble gobble.

Michael Rosen

The Thing

While I was walking down the beach one bright
   and sunny day,
I saw a great big wooden box a-floatin' in the bay.
I pulled it in and opened it up and much to my
   surprise,
Oh, I discovered a *   * right before my eyes,
Oh, I discovered a *   * right before my eyes.

I picked it up and ran to town as happy as a king,
I took it to a guy I know who'd buy most anything
But this is what he hollered at me as I walked in his
   shop:
Oh, get out of here with that *   * before I call
   a cop . . .

I turned around and got right out, a-runnin' for my
   life,
And then I took it home with me to give it to my
   wife,
But this is what she hollered at me as I walked in
   the door:
Oh, get out of here with that *   * and don't
   come back no more . . .

I wandered all around the town until I chanced to
  meet
A hobo who was looking for a handout on the
  street.
He said he'd take most any old thing, he was a
  desperate man,
But when I showed him the * * he turned
  around and ran . . .

I wandered on for many years, a victim of my fate,
Until one day I came upon Saint Peter at the gate,
And when I tried to take it inside he told me where
  to go:
Get out of here with that * * and take it
  down below . . .

The moral of the story is if you're out on the beach
And you should see a great big box and it's within
  your reach,
Don't ever stop and open it up, that's my advice to
  you,
'Cause you'll never get rid of the * * no matter
  what you do,
Oh, you'll never get rid of the * * no matter
  what you do.

Charles R. Grean

Purple People Eater

Well, I saw the thing a-comin' out of the sky,
It had one long horn and one big eye.
I commenced to shakin' and I said, 'Ooh-wee,
It looks like a Purple People Eater to me.'

It was a one-eyed, one-horned, flyin' Purple
    People Eater,
One-eyed, one-horned, flyin' Purple
    People Eater,
One-eyed, one-horned, flyin' Purple
    People Eater,
Sure looked strange to me.

Well, he came down to earth and he lit in a tree,
I said, 'Mister Purple People Eater, don't eat me.'
I heard him say in a voice so gruff,
'I wouldn't eat you 'cause you're so tough.'

Well bless my soul, rock'n roll, flyin' Purple
    People Eater,
Pidgeon-toed, under-growed, flyin' Purple
    People Eater,
He wears short shorts, friendly little
    People Eater,
What a sight to see.

I said, 'Mister Purple People Eater, what's your
    line?'
He said, 'Eatin' purple people, and it sure is fine,
But that's not the reason that I came to land,
I wanna get a job in a rock and roll band.'

    It was a one-eyed, one-horned, flyin' Purple
        People Eater,
    One-eyed, one-horned, flyin' Purple
        People Eater,
    One-eyed, one-horned, flyin' Purple
        People Eater,
    Sure looked strange to me.

And then he swung from the tree and he lit on the
    ground,
And he started to rock, a-really rockin' around.
It was a crazy ditty with a swingin' tune,
Singa bop bapa loop a lap a loom bam boom.

    Well bless my soul, rock'n roll, flyin' Purple
        People Eater.
    Pidgeon-toed, under-growed, flyin' Purple
        People Eater,
    He wears short shorts, friendly little
        People Eater,
    What a sight to see.

Well he went on his way and then what-a you
know,
I saw him last night on a tv show.
He was blowin' it out, really knockin' 'em dead.
Rock'n roll music going round in his head.

Sheb Wooley

Riotous
Relatives

Granny's in the kitchen

Granny's in the kitchen
Doing a bit of stitching,
In came a bogie man and chased granny out –
   BOO!
'Well,' said Granny, 'That's not fair!'
'Well,' said the bogie man, 'I don't care!'

Traditional chant

You don't feel itchy, Aunty, do ya?

The mosquitoes wore tuxedoes
   and the blackflies wore black ties,
The bride she was a spider
   and the groom he was a snake,
They were going to a wedding
   in my Aunt Lucy's bedding,
And she was the wedding cake.

   Glory, glory, hallelujah,
   You don't feel itchy, Aunty, do ya?
   Glory, glory, hallelujah,
   The bugs marched down the aisle.

The little honeymooners
   were nice and cozy in her bloomers,
And the guests all took their places
   in Aunt Lucy's pillowcases.
The little beasts had such a feast,
   they danced and flew and soared,
All while Aunt Lucy snored.

Traditional

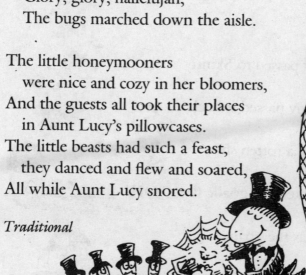

Oh, my old man's a dustman

Oh, my old man's a dustman,

He wears a dustman's hat,

He bought two thousand tickets

To see a football match.

Oh, Fatty passed to Skinny

And Skinny passed it back,

Fatty took a rotten shot

And knocked the goalie flat, OOH!

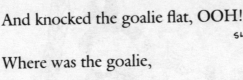

SLAP!

Where was the goalie,

When the ball was in the net?

Half way up the goalpost

With his trousers round his neck. Singing:
   Oompa oompa
   Stick it up your jumper,
   Rule Britannia, marmalade and jam,
   We threw sausages at our old man.

They put him on the stretcher,

They put him on the bed,

They rubbed his belly with a five pound jelly,

But the poor old soul was dead.

Traditional

Over the garden wall

Over the garden wall
I let my baby fall.
My mother came out,
She gave me a clout,
Over the garden wall.

Over the garden wall
I let my baby fall.
My mother came out,
She gave me a clout,
She asked me what it was all about,
Over the garden wall.

Over the garden wall
I let my baby fall,
My mother came out,
She gave me a clout,
She gave me another to match the other,
She asked me what it was all about,
Over the garden wall.

Traditional

Verbal Burble

Back chat

 Are you the guy

 That told the guy

 That I'm the guy

 Who gave the guy

 The black eye?

 No, I'm not the guy

 Who told the guy

 That you're the guy

 Who gave the guy

 The black eye.

Traditional

Says she to me

Says she to me
Is that you?
Says I, who?
Says she, you!
Says I, me?
Says she, aye.
Says I, no.
Says she, oh!
It's awfee like you.

Traditional

You remind me of a man

You remind me of a man
What man?
A man of power.
What power?
The power of hoodoo
Who do?
You do
Do what?
Remind me of a man.
What man?
A man of . . .

Traditional

Jibber jabber

Jibber jabber, gabble, babble,
Cackle, clack and prate,
Twiddle, twaddle, mutter, stutter,
Utter, splutter, blate,
Chatter, patter, tattle, prattle,
Chew the rag and crack,
Spiel and spout and spit it out,
Tell the world and quack.

Jibber, jibber jabber,
Jibber jabber, jibber jabber,
You hoo hoo hoo.
Jibber, jibber jabber,
Jibber jabber, jibber jabber,
YOU!

Sniffle, snuffle, drawl and bawl,
Snicker, snort and snap,
Bark and buzz and yap and yelp,
Chin and chirp and chat,
Shout and shoot and gargle, gasp,
Gab and gag and groan,
Hem and haw and work the jaw,
Grumble, mumble, moan.

Jibber, jibber jabber,
Jibber jabber, jibber jabber,
You hoo hoo hoo.
Jibber, jibber jabber,
Jibber jabber, jibber jabber,
YOU!

Natter, blather, yack and gas,
Waffle on and wail,
State your case and spin a yarn,
Rant and rave and rail,
Beef and bellyache and bat,
Say a mouthful, squawk,
That is what some people do
When they merely talk.

Jibber, jibber jabber,
Jibber jabber, jibber jabber,
You hoo hoo hoo.
Jibber, jibber jabber,
Jibber jabber, jibber jabber,
YOU!

Words adapted from traditional by Michael Rosen

TV dinners

How does Batman's mother call him in for tea?
  Dinner, dinner, dinner, dinner,
  Dinner, dinner, dinner, dinner, Batman!
  <small>(Batman *theme tune*)</small>

How does the Pink Panther chase insects?
  Dead ant, dead ant, dead ant, dead ant,
  dead ant . . .
  <small>(Pink Panther *theme tune*)</small>

How does Bob Marley like his doughnuts?
  Wi' jam in, jam in, and I hope you like jam in
  too.
  <small>(Jamming)</small>

Traditional

See you later, alligator

See you later, alligator
In a while, crocodile
See you later, hot potato
If you wish, jelly-fish
Not too soon, you big baboon
Toodle-oo, kangaroo
Bye-bye, butterfly
See you tomorrow, horror
In a week, freak . . .

Australian traditional

Tiffy taffy toffee

Tiffy taffy toffee
On the flee flo floor.
Tiffy taffy toffee
On the dee doe door.
Kiffy kaffy coffee
In a jig jag jug.
Kiffy kaffy coffee
In a mig mag mug.

Michael Rosen

Neverending Narratives

Busy day

Pop in pop out, pop over the road,
Pop out for a walk, pop in for a talk,
Pop down to the shop, can't stop! – pop pop
Got to pop! – pop pop, got to pop? – pop pop,
Pop where? – pop pop, pop what? – pop pop.

Pop round pop up, pop into town,
Pop out and see, pop in for tea,
Pop down to the shop, can't stop! – pop pop,
Got to pop! – pop pop, got to pop? – pop pop,
Pop where? – pop pop, pop what? – pop pop.

Michael Rosen

The flies crawl up the window

The flies crawl up the window
In sunshine and in rain;
They do not seek for pleasure,
They much prefer the pane.
And if those flies annoy you
Then here's what I advise –
Just don't have any windows
And then you will have no flies.

The flies crawl up the window,
It's all they have to do.
They go up by the thousand
And come down two by two.
The flies crawl up the window,
They say, 'We love to roam:
So once more up the window
And then we'll all go home.'

The flies crawled up the window
Then thought that they'd descend;
They all crawled for a fortnight
But didn't reach the end.
One breathless fly said, 'Blimey,
This is some window, Bill!'
It was the Crystal Palace,
So p'raps they're crawling still.

The flies crawl up the window,
It's all they have to do.
They go up by the thousand
And come down two by two.
The flies crawl up the window,
They say, 'We love to roam:
So once more up the window
And then we'll all go home.'

The flies crawl up the window
And yet the fact remains,
You'll often meet with people
Who say flies have no brains.
Next time you see flies crawling
Upside down on a shelf,
If you don't think that's clever
Just try it for yourself.

Douglas Furber

A trip to Morrow

I started on a journey just about a week ago
For the little town of Morrow in the State of Ohio.
I never was a traveller and I really didn't know
That Morrow had been ridiculed a century or so.
To Morrow, to Morrow, I have to go to Morrow,
The ticket collector told me that I have to go tomorrow.

I went down to the depot for my ticket and applied
For tips regarding Morrow, interviewed the station
   guide.
Said I, 'My friend, I want to go to Morrow and
   return
No later than tomorrow, for I haven't time to
   burn.'
To Morrow, to Morrow, I have to go to Morrow,
The ticket collector told me that I have to go tomorrow.

Said he to me, 'Now let me see, if I have heard you
   right,
You want to go to Morrow and come back
   tomorrow night,
You should have gone to Morrow yesterday and
   back today,
The train to Morrow, left at two to Morrow
   yesterday.

To Morrow, to Morrow, I have to go to Morrow,
The ticket collector told me that I have to go tomorrow.

For if you started yesterday to Morrow, don't you
    see
You should have got to Morrow and returned
    today at three.
The train that started yesterday, now understand
    me right,
Today it gets to Morrow and returns tomorrow
    night.'
To Morrow, to Morrow, I have to go to Morrow,
The ticket collector told me that I have to go tomorrow.

Said I, 'I guess you know it all, but kindly let me
    say,
How can I go to Morrow if I leave the town
    today?'
Said he, 'You cannot go to Morrow today I'll have
    you know,
For that train you see just leaving is the only one to
    go. So —
Tomorrow, tomorrow, you'll have to go tomorrow,
The train to Morrow just left today, you'll have to go
    tomorrow.

Anon

Index of first lines

We're walking through the air, 16
We three kings of Orient are, 31
Well, I saw the thing a-comin' out of the sky, 40
While I was walking down the beach one bright and
    sunny day, 38

You remind me of a man, 51

Acknowledgements

We are grateful to the following for permission to reproduce the copyright words of these songs:

Morag Blance for 'Nell and Ned' runner-up in the A & C Black Silly Song Competition.

Sheetal Borhara, Trina Bose, Sara Isenberg, Martina Klich and Rebecca Ryan of Moss Hall Junior School for 'Are you pink and green?' highly commended in the A & C Black Silly Song Competition.

Campbell Connelly & Co., Ltd for 'The biggest aspidistra in the world' by Jimmy Harper, Will Haines and Tommy Connor, © 1938 Campbell Connelly & Co Ltd, 8–9 Frith Street, London W1V 5TZ. Used by permission. All rights reserved.

Essex Music for 'The Thing' by Charles R. Grean, © 1950 (renewed) by Grean Music for the USA: administered for the USA by September Music Inc. Sub-published by Tro Music Ltd, Suite 207, Plaza 535 Kings Road, London SW10 0SZ. International copyright secured. All rights reserved. Used by permission.

International Music Publications Limited, Southend Road, Woodford Green, Essex IG8 8HN, for 'A G-nu', words by Michael Flanders, © 1974 Chappell Music Ltd, London W1Y 3FA/International Music Publications Limited; 'The flies crawled up the window' words by Douglas Furber, © 1933 Chappell Music Ltd, London W1Y 3FA/International Music Publications Limited; 'I can't do my bally bottom button up' words and music by J. P. Long, © 1916 Star Music Publishing, B. Feldman & Co Ltd, London WC2H 0EA; 'Purple People Eater' by Sheb Wooley, © 1958 Channel Music Co. USA, Peter Maurice Music Co. Ltd, London WC2H 0EA. All titles used by permission.

The Singing Kettle for their help in providing the source of 'Says she to me'.

Robert Soulsby and Class 1S, Brookvale Junior School for 'Gunerania's Wedding Cake' first prize winner in the A & C Black Silly Song Competition.

Every effort has been made to trace and acknowledge copyright owners. If any right has been omitted, the publishers offer their apologies and will rectify this in subsequent editions following notification.